The Barbadian Rum Shop

The Barbadian Rum Shop

The Other Watering Hole

Peter Laurie

Photographs by Sue Hume, Maxie Baldeo and Orlando Marville

MACMILLAN
CARIBBEAN

Macmillan Education
Between Towns Road, Oxford OX4 3PP
A division of Macmillan Publishers Limited
Companies and representatives throughout the world

www.macmillan-caribbean.com

ISBN 0 333 79390 0

First Published 2001

Designed by Stafford and Stafford
Map by Martin Sanders
Cover design by Stafford and Stafford
Cover photographs by Sue Hume and courtesy of R L Seale & Company Ltd

Printed in Hong Kong

2005 2004 2003 2002 2001
10 9 8 7 6 5 4 3 2 1

Contents

Preface

When I first thought of doing this photographic book on the rum shops of Barbados, the aim was to capture in photos what seemed to be a disappearing icon of our cultural landscape, a quintessential piece of Barbadiana threatened by the forces of modernity.

Only after I started visiting dozens of rum shops scattered across the country did I realise that the Barbadian rum shop was alive and well. True, many have fallen on hard times, barely allowing their owners to eke out an existence. Many have closed down entirely, as we illustrate in the book. But many are still doing business and some are thriving enterprises, or so I inferred; for the canny proprietors were, in true Bajan fashion, not about to admit to success.

What is clear is that the rum shop has changed and will continue to change. Those who dislike change in itself will lament this. But the fact is that the 'shop' side of the rum shop has been practically wiped out by the rise of the supermarkets and the mini-marts. No longer does it or can it serve as general store to the village. For many in the country, however, because of the flexibility of the opening hours and its accessibility on foot or bicycle, the rum shop still serves as a convenience store or corner shop.

But the 'rum' side of the rum shop has in many cases prospered. This is the rum shop as local 'pub' or bar where people – still mainly men, but increasing numbers of women as well – gather to drink, eat, talk and play games such as dominoes. Here too there has been change, and many of the popular bars bear little resemblance to the traditional rum shop. I have included them, despite their lack of architectural 'authenticity', because they seemed to me to embody the spirit of the rum shop. I have however drawn the line at mini-marts that choose to sell drinks on the side.

Many of these rum shops and bars are popular with the younger crowd – including women and a growing number of visitors to the island. They differ from the more upscale bar not only in prices but also in their relaxed and uninhibited atmosphere.

The book includes photos both of the traditional rum shops as well as of more recent or remodelled bars that evoke the spirit of the rum shop. It has a dual purpose: to document in photos and provide historical background to a unique Barbadian institution, as well as to encourage Barbadians and visitors alike to experience first hand the exuberant atmosphere of the Barbadian rum shop.

There are about a thousand rum shops in Barbados. We obviously could not include them all, but we tried to give a fair geographical balance. I am sure there are many fine ones we missed.

The first section of the book tells the fascinating story of rum. where it began, how it is made and the many ways you can drink it. The second section gives an insight into the brewing of Barbados' prize-winning beer, Banks. The third section is a brief social history of the rum shop in Barbados. The fourth and final section features some special rum shops that the reader will find more than worth a visit.

I am indebted to all those rum shop proprietors, managers and assistants who welcomed the photographers and me. They were generous with their time and information. Also thanks to the several persons who suggested rum shops worth a visit.

Thanks too to Foursquare Distillery and R. L. Seale & Co. Ltd, Mount Gay Distilleries, the West Indies Rum Distillery and Hanschell Inniss Ltd, along with Banks Breweries, for their help and co-operation in the production of this book.

Thanks personally to Henderson Carter for his valuable research assistance and to Sir David Seale, Patrick Mayers, Claire Jordan and Sophie Allsopp for providing much useful information and help.

Thanks especially to Sue Hume, Maxie Baldeo and Orlando Marville for their company and their splendid photography.

And finally, a special thanks for Pam and Christopher who at times must have thought I was crazy.

Peter Laurie

The author hard at work with his research at the Flash-N-Bar Restaurant, Pilgrim Road, Christ Church. Maxie Baldeo

1 | The Story of Rum

'There's nought, no doubt so much the spirit calms as rum and true religion'

Lord Byron, *Don Juan*, c. II 34 (1820)

'Rum, sweet rum, when yuh call Ah bound to come...'

Old-time calypso

Where de rum come from... Rum was born in Barbados in the mid-seventeenth century. But, like most truly magnificent creations, it did not have an auspicious beginning.

Our first knowledge of its existence and effect comes from Richard Ligon, a refugee from the English Civil War, who spent from 1647 to 1650 in the island, and wrote a *True and Exact History of Barbados*, published in 1657. In discussing the drinking habits of Bajans, Ligon noted with disapproval: 'The seventh sort of drink is that we make of the skimming of sugar which is infinitely strong but not very pleasant in taste. ...The people drink much of it, indeed too much; for it often layes them asleep on the ground and that is accounted a very unwholesome thing.' The name Ligon discovered for this unhealthy brew was the aptly coined Kill-Devil: 'the drink of the Island made of the skimmings of the Coppers that boyle the Sugar which they call Kill-Divell'.

However, an unknown visitor to Barbados in 1651 first mentioned the name that would stick: 'The chief fudling they make in the Island is Rumbullion, alias Kill-Divill, and this is made of sugar cane distilled: a hott hellish and terrible liquor.' Rumbullion was soon contracted to rum. And rum has remained to this day the universal name of this delightful spirit made from sugar cane.

From a drink fit only for servants and slaves to the nectar of the gods

Rum was initially considered fit only for the lower and poorer classes: small farmers and traders, sailors, servants and slaves. According to Father Labat, the French missionary, it was strong, violent and cheap, not to mention rough and disagreeable. This almost universal early reputation of rum had very little to do with its manufacture. It was due to the fact that the rum was made originally from the skimmings of the boiled sugar cane juice, which contained a number of unmentionable ingredients. Newly distilled rum, even today, has a high concentration of alcohol. It needs to be mellowed through dilution and/or ageing. These problems were solved when rum began to be made from molasses or cane juice, and when ageing was introduced.

Cutting sugar cane. Sue Hume

Indeed things were soon to change. In 1708 the historian Oldmixon noted that Barbados was the home of 'the famous spirit known as Rum which by some persons is preferred to Brandy… It is said to be very wholesome and has therefore supplied the place of Brandy in punch. Indeed it is much better than malt spirits and the sad liquor sold by our [English] distillers.' Barbados rum became the most prized of the Caribbean rums and was exported in large quantities in the eighteenth century, to become the toast of Europe and North America.

George Washington spent seven weeks in Barbados in 1751 with his brother Lawrence, who was suffering from tuberculosis. Barbados was then one of the two thriving commercial centres in the Western hemisphere – the other being Boston. The brothers were lavishly entertained and undoubtedly learned to savour the fine quality of Barbados rum. When George ran for the legislature in 1758 his agent ensured that the citizens of Frederick County, Virginia, were treated with 28 gallons of rum and 50 gallons of rum punch, most of which came from Barbados. Rum and politics have been a perennial if not always perfect mix.

Colleton sugar factory – long abandoned. Sue Hume

An old mill wall. Sue Hume

How rum is made   Rum is a distilled product of the fermented sugars obtained from various by-products of sugar manufacture. Sugar cane juice and molasses are the two most common materials. Molasses, a syrupy residue of sugar production, is the most widely used raw material. Barbados rum is made only from molasses.

A traditional distillery: West Indies Distillery. Sue Hume

A load of sugar cane ready for the factory. Sue Hume

There are two methods of distilling rum: the pot still and the continuous or column still.

Originally all rum was made in pot stills. This was a simple boiling pan in which a batch of fermented molasses mixture was heated by fire to produce heavy rums full of flavour and aroma. Modified versions of the pot still are used today to produce strongly flavoured rums.

Continuous still rum is distilled (as the name suggests) continuously instead of in batches, and the result is a rum much lighter in flavour.

The bulk of rum in Barbados is made in continuous stills at the three distilleries, but pot still rum is used – mainly to add to continuous still rum to enhance the flavour.

In addition to ethanol, the main product of fermentation, a number of organic compounds are produced that give rum its characteristic flavour and aroma. They include glycerol, aldehydes, volatile acids, esters and higher alcohols. These are collectively known as congenerics. The heavier the flavour of the rum, the higher the presence of congenerics. Rum is classified by the amounts of congenerics present.

It is advisable not to try to pronounce 'congenerics' if you have had any rum to drink.

Pot still at West Indies Distillery. Sue Hume

Inside a traditional distillery: Mount Gay Distillery. Sue Hume

Fermentation of molasses at Mount Gay Distillery. Sue Hume

The secret is in the ageing and the blending

All rum is white (colourless), when distilled. Even when aged in oak barrels, its colour is more akin to that of white wine. The brown colour of rum comes from adding a bit of caramel (burnt sugar).

Barbados rum is diluted and aged in American white oak barrels (which previously contained bourbon) holding about 40 imperial liquid gallons. Some rum producers also char the inside of the barrels to give the rum a slightly smoky flavour. The rum is allowed to mature for anywhere from six months to twelve years. The wood, being porous, lets in oxygen, which causes changes in the chemical structure of the rum. Wood also imparts tannin, which adds to the flavour.

Oak barrels of rum at Foursquare Distillery. Sue Hume

The overall effect of the wood is to make the rum wonderfully smooth and mellow. Blending refers to mixing the two basic rums produced (lightly flavoured continuous still rum and heavily flavoured pot still rum), with the occasional addition of other flavouring agents such as sherry. The difference between one blend and another depends on the proportion of rums used, the age of the different rums, and the strength at which they have matured.

The overall result of the ageing and blending is a marvellous variety of rums: rums that have a rich, mellow oak character; a light smoky aroma and subtle fruity undertones; a beautiful luminous clarity and a rich smoothness to complement their golden amber colour.

Inside an ultra-modern distillery – Foursquare Distillery. Sue Hume

A brand for every taste

Today there are three distilleries in Barbados: Foursquare Rum Distillery, Rum Refinery of Mount Gay Ltd, and West Indies Rum Distillery. The rum from these distilleries is marketed under a number of famous brands, many of which are exported. Foursquare and R. L. Seale & Co. Ltd produce Old Brigand Black Label Rum (ten-year-old premium rum), Old Brigand Rum (three to five years old), Special Barbados Rum (three to five years old), E.S.A. Field (a white rum) and Foursquare Spiced Rum. Mount Gay produces Mount Gay Extra Old (12 to 17 years old), Sugar Cane Brandy (five to seven years old), Mount Gay Eclipse (three to five years old) and Mount Gay Premium White. West Indies Rum Distillery and Hanschell Inniss Ltd produce Cockspur V.S.O.R. (a twelve-year-old premium rum), 1639 (a ten to twelve-year-old premium rum), Cockspur Old Gold (five years old), Cockspur Five Star (three years old), Cockspur White Rum and Malibu Caribbean Rum with two flavours: coconut and lime.

The distilleries welcome visitors and each has a visitor centre and organised tours.

But how do you drink it?

Premium aged rums like Mount Gay Extra Old, Cockspur V.S.O.R. and 1639, and Old Brigand Black Label should preferably be drunk like single malt whiskies: either neat, on the rocks or with a dash of water or soda water. They can also be substitutes for cognac.

Other less mature rums, both brown and white, can be mixed with a variety of soft drinks or juices, including the ingredients for the famous rum punch: one of sour (lime juice), two of sweet (sugar), three of strong

Inside Mount Gay Distillery. Sue Hume

Tasting the product: West Indies Distillery. Sue Hume

(rum), and four of weak (crushed ice), plus a dash of Angostura bitters. Hardy rum shop men toss the rum off neat and 'chase' it with water, a soft drink or even a Banks beer! Many connoisseurs use coconut water with rum. This makes a superb drink.

There are many famous drinks made from rum: cuba libre, daiquiri, zombie, pina colada, and rum sour. A classic is the Barbados rum cocktail. It is simplicity itself, but what genius: rum, a bit of sugar to taste (but definitely on the dry side), a splash of Angostura bitters and lots of crushed ice. Shake vigorously and pour into shot glasses. Drink while it still has its head and you yours, and admire the sunset or whatever.

For other drinks see the *Caribbean Rum Book* (Macmillan).

Yes, you can cook with it

Cooking with rum is fun. For a host of recipes, see *Cooking with Caribbean Rum* by Laurel-Ann Morley (Macmillan). Our own favourite recipe is the following:

Barbados Rum Cake

1 bottle of aged Barbados rum

4 cups flour

2 cups dried fruit

1 tsp. baking soda

3 large eggs

4 cups brown sugar

1 cup butter

1 pint milk

lemon juice

nuts

Before starting, sample rum to check it is of highest quality. Two shots should do nicely. Select large mixing bowl. Check rum again. Swirl it slowly in the mouth before swallowing. Beat 1 cup of butter in the bowl. Add 1 cup of rum. Before adding, hold up to the light and then slowly drink a shotglass full. Rum must be aged and very smooth and mellow.

Add 1 seaspoon of thugar and beat again. Add another cup of rum. But first drink some to ensure ish at room temperature. Add leggs, 2 cups fried druit and beat until high.

If druit gets thtuck in featers fry loose wish a drewscriber. Shample rum again. Sheck it ish of besht qua... qua... quality. Next, shift 3 cups of pepper or salt, doeshnt matter. Fold in shopped butter and strained nuts. Add 1 batlespoon of brown thugar or any damn colour. Wix mel. Grease oven. Turn cake pan to 350 gredees. Pour into boven and ache. Check rum again and if bottle ish empty, bo to ged.

Shimply murbelous!

2 | The Other Brew: Banks, the Beer of Barbados

Banks (Barbados) Breweries began operations in 1961. Its Banks beer has been a phenomenal success, winning fifteen medals at the prestigious Monde Selection brewers' quality competition since Banks began participating in 1971. The brewery won four gold medals at the most recent competition, for its beer, its Twist shandy, its Plus energy drink and its Tiger Malt.

Banks beer is the favourite of most Bajans, and the majority of its sales are to rum shops. It is no surprise, therefore, that a growing number of those shops are branded in the distinctive Banks colours of red, white and black.

There are three other Banks beer products: Banks Light, a low alcohol beer; XXTRA Strong Brew, a dark, hops-accented flavour beer with a higher alcoholic content (brewed only seasonally); and Braumeister Special, a strong-flavoured beer.

Inside Banks Brewery. Sue Hume

Banks itself is a Pilsener-type lager made from a unique blend of Australian and British malted barleys. This malted barley blend, coupled with Barbadian water that has been filtered though coral limestone, results in a smooth, fresh, effervescent taste.

The distinctive aroma of Banks comes from a mix of European and American hops, a special strain of yeast, and cane sugar added to improve fermentation and give Banks that special Bajan oomph!

In the Banks state-of-the-art laboratory, each brew is meticulously analysed at every stage of the brewing process to guarantee first-class quality.

3 | The Barbadian Rum Shop

The rum shop is a unique and ancient Barbadian institution; as ancient as the church. It is said that for every church in Barbados you will find a rum shop, sometimes close at hand. And churches abound, with every possible denomination to be found scattered across the 21 by 14 miles of this beautiful island.

Linton Bar and Grocery: a traditional rum shop in Lucas Street, St Philip. Two customers cooling out in the front. Maxie Baldeo

Proprietor Mrs Lauren Linton at her work table in the centre of the room behind the counter. Note the shelves neatly provisioned with rum and dry goods, and also the traditional glass case in which bread, cakes, cheese and other food is kept safe from flies. Maxie Baldeo

One might truly say that this is an island devoted to the spiritual and the spirituous.

In many ways the church and the rum shop were the two defining community institutions of the typical Barbadian village, the church appealing largely to the women and the rum shop to the men. Estimates of the number of rum shops today vary from as high as 5,000 to as low as 800. There are probably now about 1,000 in existence. There are two obstacles to arriving at an accurate estimate. First, counting licences to sell liquor is misleading because many other types of bars and restaurants also have liquor licences. More important, it all depends on what you mean by a rum shop.

So what exactly is a rum shop?

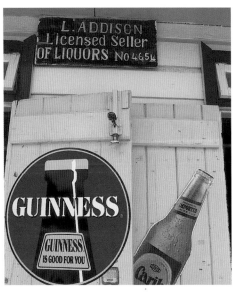

A liquor licence sign is posted outside all rum shops. Sue Hume

A view into Gitten's Cosy Nook, Roebuck Street, one of the smallest rum shops in Barbados. Sue Hume

A small traditional shop: Snagg's Shop, Black Rock Main Road, St Michael. Sue Hume

Early origins: the seventeenth-century 'Tipling House'

The origins of the rum shop might well be said to lie in the 'Tipling Houses' of the seventeenth century. These were a kind of tavern that sprang up in Bridgetown not long after the island was settled in 1627. The name 'Tipling House' was common in England from the sixteenth century to describe houses that sold intoxicating liquor. For example, an English Act of 1552 speaks in the preamble of 'Comen Ale-houses and other houses called Tiplinge houses'. The Tipling Houses in Barbados were very popular and did a roaring trade in rum and other spirits that soon caught the attention and earned the disapproval of the authorities.

The early colonists were, by all accounts, hard drinkers. It was estimated that each white male settler drank 26 gallons of rum a

Replica of a traditional shop at Tyrol Cot Village, Codrington Hill, St Michael. Courtesy of the National Trust

year; free blacks and coloured 20 gallons; and slaves 3 gallons. Presumably the difference in consumption depended on the amount of leisure available to each class of persons.

One early English Governor, Joseph West, sniffily observed that 'one English servant is worth two Barbadians, they are so much addicted to rum, that they will do little but while the bottle is at their nose.'

In 1652 an Act was passed by the Assembly 'prohibiting persons from keeping a common alehouse or Tipling, selling any liquor of this country's spirit to be drank in ye houses or plantations without licence'. This was followed in 1654 by another Act to suppress the unlicensed rum houses. The problem was, from the authorities' point of view, that the distillation and sale of rum was open to just about anyone who wanted to get into the business. The Assembly, however, wanted to bring the manufacture and sale of rum under the control of the plantations.

In 1668 legislation was passed 'preventing the selling of Brandy and Rum in Tipling Houses near the Broad Paths and Highways within this Island'. It provided that 'No persons within the Island, shall be permitted to keep any stills for Distilling of Rum, except such persons as have lands or canes of their own, or such as keep refineries.'

The 1668 law was intended not only to control the manufacture and sale of rum, but also to curb the disorderly behaviour that the Tipling Houses apparently encouraged. The preamble to the Act had this to say:

intolerable Hurts and Troubles to this Island do continually grow and increase through the Multiplicity of such abuses and disorders as are daily had and used in unlicensed Tipling Houses... On the sabbath days many lewd, lose and idle people do resort to such Tipling Houses, who by their drunkenness, swearing, and other miscarriages, do, in a very high nature, blaspheme the name of God, prophane the sabbath, and bring scandal upon the christian religion.

Church and rum shop in conflict! In other words, officialdom, as usual, simply wanted to stop ordinary people having a good time. The planters and merchants could cavort in the privacy of their own homes (and cavort they did) but for the lower orders – whites, free coloured, black slaves and seamen – to engage in such conduct was deemed scandalous. Moreover, many of the Tipling Houses were owned by free coloured, a further cause for suppression.

Barbados was unique in the development of rum and the Tipling House. Thomas Walduck, writing in 1708, noted the different thrusts of European colonisation: the Spanish set up churches, the Dutch set up trading stations and the English created Tipling Houses.

Chalky Mount Bar, St Andrew – the highest rum shop in Barbados? Sue Hume

Opposite: Payne Bar and Grocery, Cave Hill main road, St Michael – ancient and ravaged by time, but still going. Sue Hume

Inside D. and J. Variety. Sue Hume

A different type of rum shop: a wayside bar with an attached shed for games and drinking at D. and J. Variety, Coach Hill, St John. Sue Hume

The rise of the village shop

The Tipling Houses of the seventeenth century were the precursors of the modern rum shop, in that they were popular and frequented primarily by the lower orders. But it was the emergence of the urban and rural villages – mainly after Emancipation – that gave rise to the village shop, which was a combination of grocery and bar, the defining feature of the classic rum shop.

Barbados, being a very small island almost totally cultivated from as early as the seventeenth century, was so dominated by the sugar plantations that even after Emancipation most of the freed slaves had to continue living in the tenantries attached to the plantations.

Despite the dominance of the plantations, freehold villages did emerge. The earliest type was the poorer white settlement of peasant proprietors, fishermen, artisans and shopkeepers, with a scattering of free coloured and blacks. These villages were located primarily on the eastern side of the island, from Foul Bay in St Philip to Pie Corner in St Lucy. They still exist, but are now no longer white, owing to a process of interbreeding and white emigration. A good example is St Elizabeth's village in St Joseph.

The second oldest type was the pre-Emancipation free black village on land endowed by planters' wills. These villages grew larger after Emancipation as freed slaves gravitated to them and villagers bought land from adjoining plantations. An example of this type of free village is Sweet Bottom (now out of prudery renamed Sweet Vale) in St George, dating from 1777.

The latest type of village arose after Emancipation as freed blacks who had

E. Lucas Shop, Weston, St James – a shop which still does well on the convenience side. Sue Hume

accumulated money bought marginal lands of plantations. Examples of these early post-Emancipation villages are Rock Hall, Workman's, Black Rock and Cave Hill.

In the second half of the nineteenth century the growth and spread of villages was greatly helped by the depression of the world market for sugar and the resulting subdivision and sale of indebted plantations by white speculators to workers. Some 70 new villages arose between 1850 and 1880. This trend continued into the twentieth century, with some 60 new villages being created in the first three decades, alongside the expansion of older villages and the growth of urban tenantries. Much of this process was spurred by the over $10 million sent back or brought back by some 50,000 Barbadian emigrants to the USA and Panama.

It was these villages that defined the shape of working class life in Barbados and that also served as the breeding ground for the nascent black middle class. And it was in these villages that one of the important communal institutions of life in Barbados developed: the village shop.

Historic facade in Speightstown: Jackie's Cash 'N' Carry. **Maxie Baldeo**

Retail selling had been an important activity even during slavery, when female hawkers and hucksters sold vegetables and ground provisions. After Emancipation the more successful itinerant vendors became shopkeepers. Other shops started as peddling shops, where the owners would sell small items from their homes, usually transacting business though a side window.

Black property owners also set up shops to diversify their activity. Many a small entrepreneur used 'Panama' money to open a shop. In addition to the independent shopkeepers, the Bridgetown merchants began either to start shops themselves or to assist others in setting up shops for which they provided goods on consignment for sale. Names like Proverbs, Cole, Taylor, Pitcher Connel, Ince & Co. Ltd, Cheeseman, Sampson, R. L. Seale and Emtage were those of prominent provision merchants. James A. Tudor, a black businessman, father of Sir James Tudor the eminent politician, owned a string of shops throughout Barbados. The two major wholesalers today are R. L. Seale and M. E. R. Bourne.

Mum's Variety and Bar, Bayland, St Michael. Sue Hume

Boo's Shop, Hall's Road, St Michael – a popular place. Sue Hume

Many of the early shopkeepers were women, either working alongside their spouses or independently. Indeed today most of the people who own or manage rum shops are women. One of the best-known female black entrepreneurs, Mrs Rock, owner of the Rocklyn Bus Company, started as a shopkeeper in one of James A. Tudor's shops in St Andrew.

Writing in 1909, H. H. McLellan observed of the Barbadian shopkeeper: 'The Barbados shopkeeper is the liveliest, most energetic and alert man on earth. The opportunity to make half a crown excites him as if besides himself there is an electric eel in his breeches.' He goes on:

He must own a pony and cart to freight his goods from Bridgetown… From remote parts of the island, fifteen miles or even further off from Bridgetown, these tough little ponies haul the carts to town and haul them back the same day, freighted with goods, toiling up stiff climbs with a splendid pluck… and never needing any encouragement from the shopkeepers, who sit in the carts and utilise these spare moments in plotting against their untoward and oppressive fate.

Mrs Effie Henry of Effie's Bar and Grocery, Upper Station Hill, St Michael. Sue Hume

The dual role of the village rum shop

What makes the rum shop unique is its dual function: grocery store on the one hand, and tavern or bar on the other. It is as if in the American Wild West the general store and the saloon were one and the same place. In fact most rum shops carried the name of the proprietor followed by 'bar and grocery'.

Patrons at Effie's Bar and Grocery, Upper Station Hill, St Michael. Sue Hume

The rum shop as grocery store

As a grocery store the rum shop played a vital role, in the era before supermarkets and effective private or public transport, in providing the necessities of life to the residents of the village. Shops were usually located at one of the four crossroads in a village or strategically placed at the entrance or exit to a village. They were therefore always within walking distance of their customers. A village's importance was often assessed by the number of shops in it.

The shopkeeper usually bought items in bulk and measured out the quantities to be sold. These were stored in wooden barrels or crocus bags (burlap sacks). One of the essential items in a shop, still to be seen occasionally today, was the traditional weighing scale with its removable pan and weights. This was used for measuring items like potatoes, onions, sugar, corn meal, salted fish and animal feed. The amount sold would then be wrapped in brown paper. Foodstuffs like cheese, bread, 'lead pipes' (a long, hard, sweet bread) and fish cakes were usually kept in a glass case on top of the counter to keep insects away. In many rum shops today you will still see these glass cases being used for storing food.

Bragg's Hill Shop, St Joseph – a traditional rural rum shop which still survives by selling goods. Sue Hume

A typical glass case on the counter at Gagg's Hill Shop, Joe's River, St Joseph. Sue Hume

Mr R. Brathwaite, proprietor of Bragg's Hill Shop. Sue Hume

Old weighing scales still in use at Goodridge Bar and Grocery, Martins Bay, St John. Sue Hume

Beverages were kept in an ice-box. Blocks of ice weighing 50 pounds were delivered every day or every other day. Liquids like 'lard oil', kerosene oil and rum would be measured in 'pots' of which there were half-gill, half-pint, pint, half-gallon and gallon measurements. In most cases the customer brought her own receptacle. The waste generated by individual packaging and plastic bags today was unknown then.

A typical rum shop facade: Bovell's Place, Baxter's Road, Bridgetown. Sue Hume

The rum shop had characteristic architectural features. A basic chattel house design was fronted by a façade of three doors from which one or two steps led down to the road. A hood over the steps usually provided protection from sun and rain. Set back about 5 feet from the entrance was a wooden counter running the length of the shop. Under the counter was storage space for barrels and sacks. Around the back and sides of the shop were shelves on which goods were kept and displayed, including various brands of rum. Usually in the middle of the room behind the counter was a table where the shopkeeper kept the cash till and the credit book. Female shopkeepers often kept the proceeds of the day's sales in several cigarette tins – one for sweet drinks, one for cigarettes, and so on. They would also have several pockets under their skirts where they kept the cash used to buy stock.

Behind the shop was often the living quarters of the shopkeeper's family. One side of the shop, usually separated by a partition, was set aside for the bar. Behind that might be a more private room – a mini-saloon, if you like, where customers could sit around a table and drink and play cards, dominoes or draughts.

An old rural rum shop still struggling with the sale of groceries: Rudder's Shop, Coffee Gully, St Joseph. Sue Hume

Barclays Park. Sue Hume

Apart from providing groceries and general provisions, the village shop also served in many respects as a village bank, through the informal system of credit that it made available to its customers. In fact most of the sales of the shop were based on credit, as were its purchases. It was common for a customer to credit goods from the shopkeeper until pay day or until a pig or sheep was butchered and sold. The credit transaction was not based on a written agreement. Neither bill nor invoice was given, nor did the customer sign anything.

The shopkeeper simply noted down the amount due in a book. For this reason the system was known as 'trust'. The shop was also the place where school children had their lunch before the advent of free school meals. These lunches were also 'trusted'.

Many shopkeepers ran into difficulties with the trust system, so that a common sign posted in shops was: 'Trust dead; bad pay kill he'; or 'No credit today; come back tomorrow'; or 'Credit given to people over 90 years of age, accompanied by their grandmother'. The system of informal credit no longer exists today, except in rare instances. But in the hard times of yesteryear when families were large and agricultural wages were low (28 cents a day for men and 20 cents for women in the 1930s), it ensured that many a family survived.

Proprietor Leroy Hall, still persisting after decades.
Sue Hume

Headley Shop, Horse Hill, St Joseph. Sue Hume

The rum shop as bar and tavern

Skeete's Beach Bar, Martins Bay, St John, shows the evolution of the rum shop as a bar. Sue Hume

The other role of the rum shop was to be the local tavern or 'pub' in a village. For this purpose it had an area set apart for the bar, usually at the side of the shop with its own entrance, where the men gathered to drink and talk and play games such as dominoes, draughts and cards. Sometimes there would be a larger back room with tables and benches. The men would also buy corned beef or sardines and biscuits to eat while they drank. Some rum shops traditionally reserved, like an English pub, the back room with its table and chairs for the more 'respectable' white-collar members of the village, while the hardier working-class folk downed their snaps on their feet in the public side of the bar, sometimes chewing on a hot pepper first.

Before the development of modern centralised distillation, many rum shop proprietors used to buy their rum in barrels from nearby plantations and do their own blending. They would keep this rum in a demi-john (a large, wicker-covered bottle holding up to 10 gallons). Purchases were made in 'snaps', half-gill and gill pots, which were tossed down and 'chased' with water.

Ward Bar and Grocery, Sargeant Street, St John: a small, breezy bar tucked away in the hill. Maxie Baldeo

After the centralisaton of distillation in two or three large distilleries, the Bridgetown merchants used to buy in bulk from the distilleries, blend in their own vats, and bottle their own brands such as Proverb's 'Pretty Girl', Doorly's 'Macaw', Cave Shepherd's 'Coral Land', Goddard's 'Gold Braid', Hanschell's 'Cockspur', Alleyne Arthur's 'Special' and Mount Gay's 'Eclipse'. These were all available in rum shops. One of the most popular of shop rums is E.S.A. Field White Rum (commonly and irreverently referred to as eternal saviour and friend).

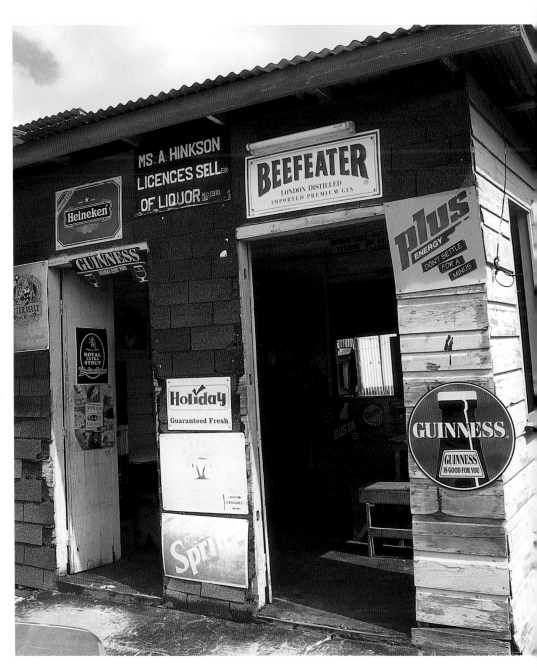

Angie's Bar, Spooners Hill, St Michael. Sue Hume

Inside Buffy's Bar, Inch Marlowe, Christ Church. **Maxie Baldeo**

Inside Vernon's Cosy Bar, Bridgetown. Sue Hume

The subsequent rise of the supermarkets in the 1950s caused a shake-up in the Bridgetown wholesale merchant business. Many merchants went out of business. Several consolidated. Many switched from selling in bulk to selling branded products. This had an effect on the production of branded rums. Today there are only three rum producers: Mount Gay Rum Distilleries, which blends and bottles the Mount Gay brands from rum produced by the Mount Gay refinery; Hanschell Inniss Ltd, which blends and bottles the Cockspur brands from rum produced by the West Indies Rum Distillery; and R. L. Seale & Co., which blends and bottles the Old Brigand and Alleyne Arthur brands from rum produced by Foursquare Distillery.

Pug's Bar and Restaurant, opposite the airport, Christ Church. Maxie Baldeo

The O'Neal Shop, Pie Corner, St Lucy. Sue Hume

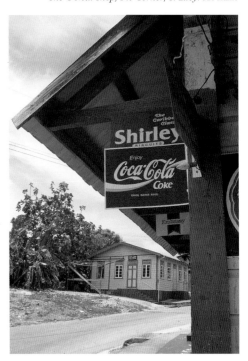

Flash-N-Bar Restaurant, Pilgrim Road, Christ Church. **Maxie Baldeo**

Rum today is usually bought in shops in 'flasks' or 'minis'. Nowadays, beer is drunk probably more than rum, especially by younger men and women, with Banks and Heineken being the most popular choices.

Men came to the rum shops not only to drink and eat, but also to discuss politics and cricket and other hot topics of the day, to gossip and play games and enjoy each other's company, or simply to 'lime', that typically Caribbean way of passing the time without any clear purpose. The most popular games were – and still are – dominoes, draughts and cards. Sometimes, if the shop did not have a back room for players the men would play under the street light in front of the shop.

Trottie's Bar, Boarded Hall, St George. Maxie Baldeo

Draughts – one of the most popular rum shop games; White's Bar, Speightstown. Maxie Baldeo

The rum shop as community centre

Because of its important dual functions as general store and tavern the rum shop developed as a natural community centre in the days before officially organised community activities. It was the obvious place for both men and women to go to get news and to give news; to meet their neighbours and socialise. In the early days of television, the rum shop was one of the few houses in a village which could afford a television set, so that people would often go there to watch it. Domino and whist tournaments, pitting one village against another, would be organised and held in rum shops. Jukeboxes provided musical entertainment and dancing for the younger set.

The shopkeeper was usually held in high esteem in a village. Some were influential enough to have a location named after them, such as Barnett Corner and Gaskin Hill. The shopkeeper probably knew more about the residents of the village than anyone else.

Visitors enjoying a rum shop lime at the Lime Rum Shop, St Philip. Orlando Marville

*Outside Bovell's Place,
Baxter's Road, Bridgetown.*
Sue Hume

Typical rum shop signs. Sue Hume

Nellie's Nest, Benthams, St Lucy. Sue Hume

Nellie. Sue Hume

Rum shops were also important in the politics of Barbados, especially as the franchise was gradually extended during the 1940s, eventually ending in universal adult suffrage in 1950. Candidates were expected to patronise the shops and pay for rum and corned beef and biscuits. Many a rum shop became an unofficial campaign headquarters, especially in rural areas. And shopkeepers, because of the credit they held, could be influential in the way their customers cast their votes. Shopkeepers would put up posters of the leader of the party they supported as well as a poster of the party candidate for the constituency. Many political meetings were held in front of or near the shop whose proprietor supported the party. Shopkeepers would usually supply electricity to the party of their choice during a political meeting.

Inside the Crocodile's Den, St James.
Maxie Baldeo

By the Soup Bowl, Bathsheba. Sue Hume

The rum shop today

The rum shop today has changed, and, in many respects, radically. The most devastating blow to the rum shops came from the rise of supermarkets in the 1950s, and later the growth of mini-marts. These could buy in bulk and thereby sell at lower prices, advertised heavily and offered the attraction of air-conditioned self-service. This, coupled with the increased availability of private cars and more effective public transport, meant that people no longer bought the bulk of their groceries at rum shops, only odd items they might run out of. One of the rum shops featured in this book is right opposite a supermarket, next to a mini-mart and an auto-mart run by the gas station.

Casualty Bar, Martindales Road, Bridgetown, opposite the hospital. Orlando Marville

As a result many rum shops simply went out of business and closed down, especially those that were marginally successful to start with. Several rum shops became mini-marts – some retaining the bar on the side. A few even became small supermarkets.

Rum shops today come in all shapes and sizes: Ann's Place, East Coast Road, St Andrew. Sue Hume

The unfortunate end for many a rum shop: Pilgrim Choice Bar, Newbury, St George, now closed. Sue Hume

Others stopped selling groceries, and became convenience or variety stores, stocking certain essential items that people might run out of, and, in rural areas, animal feed. But, unlike the mini-marts they did not offer self-service, although they provided a bar. The advantage they had over the supermarkets and mini-marts in this respect was that even when they were officially closed, in an emergency a knock at the window would get you the item you wanted. Even these are now suffering competition from the more recent phenomenon of the 24-hour auto-marts provided by several gas stations.

Corbin's Bar and Grocery has been at Thorpe's Corner, Holder's Hill, for generations. It is a bastion of respectability. Note the absence of advertising on the exterior, and the clean and tidy interior. Incidentally, Corbin's serves the best fish cakes in Barbados. Sue Hume

Other rum shops have become almost exclusively bars, usually providing more tables and chairs as well as a pool table, darts, slot machines and even video games to attract drinking customers. Several offer karaoke or 'golden oldies' nights on the jukebox. Many rum shops have become bars and quasi-restaurants offering a variety of typically Barbadian cooked foods to be eaten there or taken away.

These include barbecued chicken, pork chops, fish, rice and stew, fish cakes, and gizzard, ham, cheese and fish cutters (a large bread roll split open and used as a sandwich). Quite frequently they also sell pudding (pig's intestine stuffed with cooked sweet potato and blood) and souse (pig's head and feet boiled, cut up and pickled in lime juice, salt, onion and pepper) on Saturdays. Many rum shops located near to a large business enterprise do a thriving business providing hot lunches on a daily basis to employees.

Fan and menu at Gagg's Hill Shop, Joe's River, St Joseph.
Sue Hume

De Banks Garden, Bayfield, St Philip – popular for its barbecued pig tails. Maxie Baldeo

Barman with watermelon. Sue Hume

Smith's Supermarket, Belleplaine, St Andrew. Sue Hume

Almost without exception the rum shop does not advertise. It can rarely afford to. It survives by word of mouth. Most have their bunch of regulars who are going to be there on Friday and Saturday nights come hell or high water. This success is achieved by providing good food and drink, and a relaxed atmosphere.

Gen-G's Place, Palmers, St John, located a stone's throw from Codrington College. Proprietor Paula Gobin whips up delicious food on the weekends. Maxie Baldeo

Many rum shops are now painted in the bright colours of the rum and beer manufacturers.

This brings us back to the question, what exactly is a rum shop? The best answer is that you know you are in rum shop:

When you order rum by the bottle and not the glass;
When the ice comes in a plastic container;
When a Banks beer cost $2 or less;
When you drink beer from the bottle;
When nobody is sipping a glass of wine;
When there is no waiter service;
When you see a cutter or a 'lead pipe' in a glass case;
When everybody is talking at the top of their voices;
When golden oldies are playing on the jukebox;
When dominoes are being loudly slammed in the background.

Or something like that! Cheers!

Rum shop facade in Guinness decor. Sue Hume

When you really want to play dominoes, you'll find a place. Orlando Marville

Will this shop be ours one day? Doreen's shop, Black Rock Main Road, St Michael. Sue Hume

The future of the rum shop

The traditional rum shop has changed and was bound to change. It is quite pointless to lament that. Its role as a grocery was simply replaced by the supermarket and the mini-mart. But the rum shop has survived as a convenience or variety store and, more fundamentally, as a bar despite the proliferation of hundreds of sophisticated bars catering to the better-off Barbadian and tourists. The reasons for this persistence are not hard to find. They are rooted in the essentially humble nature of the institution.

No entry sign outside Boo's Shop, Hall's Road, St Michael. Sue Hume

The rum shop has suffered over the years from an 'image' problem. Stereotypes of toothless old geezers gathering at the rum shop at six in the morning to 'fire one' have continued to typify the rum shop in the middle-class imagination. 'Rum shop politics' and a 'rum shop lawyer' are pejorative terms. A rum shop is still seen in certain quarters as a place where a woman might only venture if she were not afraid of being taken for a 'woman of easy virtue'. The truth is far from these stereotypes. While the rum shop is still basically a working-class institution – and therein lie its strengths – it is literally open to and frequented by one and all.

The rum shop is plain, unvarnished and unpretentious. It says: take me as I am or don't take me at all. If you want to put on airs or have pretensions to be better than your equals, feel free to go elsewhere.

'Heavy Roller's' place, Fortescue, St Philip. People come from all over to lime in this bar. **Maxie Baldeo**

Proprietor 'Heavy Roller' behind his bar. **Maxie Baldeo**

A rum shop lime, in a typical built-on verandah. Customers outside Wharton Bar and Grocery, Padmore Village, St Philip. **Maxie Baldeo**

At the same time the rum shop is highly influential, if at times somewhat arbitrary, in setting consumption trends in the rum and beer industry. A particular brand of rum only has to be perceived, rightly or wrongly, as 'green' and the word will spread like wildfire throughout the rum shop world. Rum manufacturers depend on the rum shop for a good part of their sales. Proper rum shop bottle sizes are the 200ml, the 301ml (unique to the rum shop) and the 375ml.

The rum shop provides a relaxed, uninhibited and, at times, a refreshingly boisterous atmosphere. As in a pub you find yourself easily striking up a conversation with other patrons. You can 'free yourself up' and 'express yourself'. Everyone voices their opinions loudly, sometimes without deleting expletives, on any subject. If this offends you, feel free to go elsewhere.

The rum shop welcomes one and all. British actress Minnie Driver, in a cover story in an American Airlines in-flight magazine, admitted that one of her favourite things to do in Barbados was to visit rum shops. They used to be the preserve of middle-aged and

At Nigel Benn Aunty Bar, Shorey Village, St Andrew. Sue Hume

Opposite: Patrons at the bar at Eulene's. Maxie Baldeo

C. M. Bar and Grocery, off Massiah Street, St John; famous for lunches and for pudding and souse on Saturday. Sue Hume

At Payne Bar and Grocery, Cave Hill main road, St Michael. Sue Hume

Typical rum shop bottle sizes: a mini, flask and pint: proprietor Peter Morgan with the author at Jackie's Cash 'N' Carry, Speightstown. Maxie Baldeo

older working men. Now old and young, men and women of all classes and increasing numbers of visitors can be found rubbing shoulders in some popular rum shops. Some don't even drink alcohol. The one rule: you don't interfere with me; I don't interfere with you. If you don't like that, feel free to go elsewhere.

The rum shop offers tremendous value for money. Some of the cheapest, most delicious and authentic Barbadian food is found in rum shops. The drinks are a quarter of the cost of those in a sophisticated bar (sophistication, though only skin-deep, is always costly). If you don't like that, feel free to go elsewhere.

Playing pool in White's Bar, Speightstown. Maxie Baldeo

Savouring the rum shop atmosphere at Oistins.
Orlando Marville

Most of all the rum shop allows you to meet some very interesting people and pass a pleasant time in congenial company. If you don't like that…you're a fool.

Do you want to help someone celebrate a birthday or anniversary in a fun way without it costing you an arm and a leg? Organise with a rum shop in advance to lay on some food and take your party there.

If you're a visitor to the island, you should not miss out on the rum shop experience. While driving around the island, stop and have a drink and a bite to eat and meet another side of Barbados.

Some of the rum shops of tomorrow will look nothing like the rum shops of yesteryear or even today. But they will still be rum shops because they embody and evoke the spirit of the rum shop.

'No matter how long the world lasts, the rum shop will go on' (anonymous interviewee recorded by researchers Janet Stoute and Kenneth Ifill). I am inclined to agree.

Menu at Gitten's Cosy Nook. Sue Hume

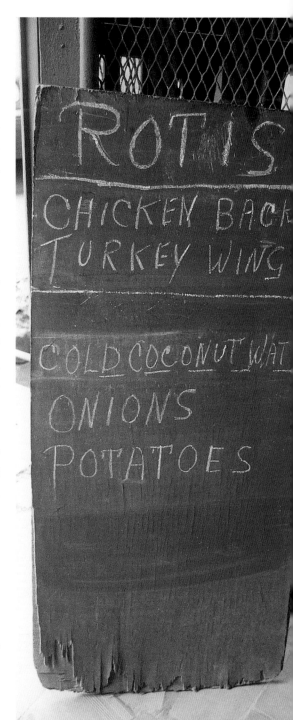

Men liming outside White's Bar, Speightstown, St Peter. Maxie Baldeo

4 | Featured Rum Shops

The following rum shops are those we discovered in the course of driving round the island to take the photos for this book, or were ones specially recommended by friends. In any event they were ones we felt we would definitely like to visit again. We could not include all that fell into this category, so these must be taken as only a sample. There are scores of fascinating rum shops offering good value for money and delightful atmosphere. Readers should check out the other rum shops mentioned elsewhere in the book, as well as go exploring for different ones.

It's hard to say what they have in common other than good locations. In fact it's their uniqueness that makes them special. Some are very much the traditional rum shop. Others would hardly be described architecturally as rum shops at all. But all embody the spirit of the rum shop.

Opposite: Winross Variety and Snack Bar, Nesfield, St Lucy. A new venture by proprietor Winston Hinds, the shop is a combination variety, mini-mart and restaurant and bar. It serves a mouth-watering array of foods including barbecued chicken, rice and stew, fish and chips, fish cakes and cutters. Is this venture the possible future for the rum shop? Sue Hume

Marjorie's Bar
Westbury Road, St Michael

This rum shop, located obliquely opposite the main gates of Westbury Cemetery, is a favourite 'haunt' of those attending funerals. But it's also a popular watering hole frequented by persons from all over.

This is probably the only rum shop in Barbados that serves buljol, that delicious concoction of salted fish, tomatoes, onions, peppers and salad oil. The food also includes ham, cheese and gizzard cutters.

Marjorie Morris, the proprietor, makes you feel especially welcome. There is a jukebox and Friday night is a good time to catch some golden oldies while playing dominoes.

Weekends are peak times, but any old time is a good time at Marjorie's.

Marjorie behind the counter. Sue Hume

Marjorie's Bar, Westbury Road, St Michael. Sue Hume

Inside Marjorie's Bar. Sue Hume

R. A. Mapp's Bar and Grocery
Eagle Hall Corner, St Michael

Located at the busy Eagle Hall intersection, this traditional rum shop, painted in the red and white colours of Banks beer, is hard to miss. And you shouldn't miss it.

Spacious and breezy, this is one of the largest rum shops in Barbados.

Host Kennedy Leacock, the grandson of the late Richard Mapp, the original proprietor, keeps his many patrons happy with his variety of drinks and his barbecued chicken.

Peak time is any time, but weekends are liveliest. Draughts is a favourite game and cricket and football are always hot topics.

This rum shop has been at the Eagle Hall corner for over fifty years, and you just know that it will be still there in another fifty.

Host Kennedy Leacock and a customer taking five. Sue Hume

A classic rum shop exterior. Sue Hume

Propping up the bar at R. A. Mapp's. Sue Hume

Pink Star Restaurant and Bar
Baxter's Road, Bridgetown

Despite the decline in the last decade of Baxter's Road as the favourite nightspot in Barbados, the Pink Star Restaurant and Bar at the top of Baxter's Road is still thriving.

Owned by Vanjoyce Mings, this rum shop opens until the wee hours of the morning and is a great place to end a night on the town.

The front of the building is in traditional rum shop style, and behind is a large room with tables and chairs. It has been there for over fifty years.

The food is terrific and includes fish of all kinds, rice and stew and a variety of cutters. (Try the gizzard cutter!)

When Baxter's Road is revitalised under the Bridgetown rehabilitation project, the Pink Star will remain one of the highlights.

The Pink Star Bar and Restaurant, Baxter's Road, Bridgetown. Sue Hume

Old City Bar
Palmetto Square, Bridgetown

In the heart of Bridgetown, behind Parliament in one of the busiest squares, the Old City Bar is an institution in its own right. It has stood on this corner location for over a hundred years and has witnessed many a vigorous debate continue beyond the hallowed precincts of Parliament.

One of the largest run shops, it has changed ownership over the years and is currently owned by Stephen St Hill, in whose family it has been since the 1930s.

It continues to be a great watering hole which serves a variety of delicious food including chicken, fish, fish cakes and cutters. It is a popular lunch venue, but you will find patrons there from early in the morning.

When you're in town, check it out.

Inside the Old City Bar. Sue Hume

The Old City Bar, Palmetto Square, Bridgetown, with Parliament in the background. Sue Hume

Parliament as seen from the Old City Bar. Sue Hume

73

Vernon's Cosy Bar
St Michael's Row, Bridgetown

Over a hundred years old, Vernon's Cosy Bar, owned by Joyce Knight, still nestles at the corner of St Michael's Row and Crumpton Street.

Very much in the classic rum shop mould, it is a city landmark. Morning, noon and night, Vernon's caters to a wide variety of clientele, including workers in the adjoining Queen's Park, locals from Church Village and tourists strolling through the city.

It has a jukebox and now functions mainly as a bar. If you are in the neighbourhood it's definitely worth dropping in for a cool one.

Vernon's: a traditional rum shop facade now painted in Heineken colours. Sue Hume

Vernon's Cosy Bar, St Michael's Row, Bridgetown, with the Central Bank in the background. Sue Hume

Customer at Vernon's Cosy Bar. Sue Hume

'Firing one' at Vernon's Cosy Bar. Sue Hume

Yellow Bird Bar
Corner of Bay Street and Dunlow Lane, St Michael

Whether you are heading in or out of Bridgetown along Bay Street, the Yellow Bird is a good place to stop for a cool drink or a snack.

Run by an enterprising young woman, Veronica Germain, the brightly painted Yellow Bird offers chicken and fish, fish cakes and cutters to a wide variety of clients ranging from the residents of Dunlow Lane to passers-by.

This rum shop stays opens late (2 or 3 a.m.) and is especially bustling at weekends. It has to be one of the smallest rum shops in Barbados.

Yellow Bird Bar, Bay Street, St Michael. Sue Hume

Hostess Veronica Germain behind the bar. Sue Hume

Yellow Bird: the smallest rum shop in Barbados? Sue Hume

A typical glass case for food on the counter. Sue Hume

Grant's Shop
Corner of Chelsea Road and Dalkeith Road by North Gate, Garrison, St Michael

Perched solidly on an outcrop of rock at this busy corner, Grant's Shop, now owned by Trevor Grant, has been around for over eighty years.

It is architecturally in the classic rum shop mould, even though it is now brightly painted in the green and white colours of Heineken beer. It is fronted by a set of steps that are ideal for 'liming' in the cool hours of the evening. It has a spacious back room for those who care to relax in greater comfort.

Grant's has a wide range of customers and is particularly popular with the younger set on weekends. Situated a stone's throw from the race track at the Garrison, this is one rum shop that is frequented by the racing fraternity.

Genial host Trevor Grant ensures that his customers enjoy a variety of mouth-watering food, including his famous pork cutters.

Trevor Grant, proprietor. Sue Hume

Inside Grant's Shop. Sue Hume

A cool brew. Sue Hume

Grant's Shop at the corner of Chelsea Road and the Garrison, St Michael: a classic rum shop facade. Sue Hume

Fergus' Bar
Corner of Two Mile Hill and Chapel Gap, St Michael

If you're attending a meeting at Sherbourne Conference Centre and all those speeches have you thirsty, just pop up the road to Fergus' Bar at the corner of Chapel Gap and Two Mile Hill.

This shop, originally owned by rum manufacturer Alleyne Arthur, has been at this strategic location just below the Bussa roundabout for over a hundred years. It is a traditional rum shop with three doors, a hood over the steps and a counter running the length of the shop.

Proprietor Loretta Fergus serves some of the best fish cakes you're likely to taste, as well as a variety of cutters.

Painted in the red and white colours of Banks beer, Fergus' Bar is a natural magnet for thirsty passers-by, and a popular watering hole.

Inside Fergus' Bar. Sue Hume

One and All Bar
Charles Rowe Bridge, St George

As the name implies, one and all are welcome at Beryl Walcott's rum shop located at Charles Rowe Bridge just as you turn the corner to go up to St George's Parish Church.

If you're heading out into the country it's a good place to stop to refresh yourself or have a quick bite to eat.

Painted in the characteristic red, yellow and black colours of Mount Gay rum, this has been a traditional rum shop for over fifty years.

It serves cutters and the usual variety of drinks. Friday evenings are the busiest time. Check it out.

Traditional glass case and weighing scales still adorn the counter at the One and All Bar. Sue Hume

One and All Bar, Charles Rowe Bridge, St George. Sue Hume

The side room at the One and All Bar. Sue Hume

Bascombe's Bar
Four Cross Roads, St John

If you're driving to St John's Church or Bath Beach, you can't miss Bascombe's Bar at Four Cross Roads, St John, opposite the post office and next to the Texaco gas station.

This traditional rum shop, now converted to a bar, has been in the Bascombe family for over fifty years. Painted in the red, yellow and black Mount Gay rum colours, the shop has a great set of steps for those wanting to cool out in the evening. There's always a boisterous game of dominoes going on inside the shop.

Bascombe's Bar serves lunches daily including rice and stew, chicken, fish, fish cakes and ham and cheese cutters. The food is delicious and the company always good.

Bascombe's attracts thirsty and hungry travellers, locals and tourists. Don't miss it.

Bascombe's Bar, Four Cross Roads, St John. Sue Hume

Inside Bascombe's Bar. Sue Hume

Slamming dominoes at Bascombe's Bar. Sue Hume

Gagg's Hill Shop
Joe's River, St Joseph

This shop is a popular place to stop for those travelling to Bathsheba or the East Coast. Strategically located opposite St Elizabeth's Park at the junction of Joe's River and the hill leading to the East Coast Road, it attracts visitors and locals alike.

Host Carl Mayers serves chicken, fish and pork on weekends, and cutters can be had any time. Friday is the liveliest time but the shop always seems to have customers. There is a jukebox, and cards are regularly played. Cricket, politics and boxing dominate most conversations.

Gagg's Hill Shop has been in this spot for over seventy years and will no doubt still be there in another seventy.

Carl Mayers, proprietor of Gagg's Hill Shop. Sue Hume

You know you are in a rum shop when the liquor you order is by the bottle: Gagg's Hill Shop. Sue Hume

The jukebox at Gagg's Hill Shop. Sue Hume

A classic rum shop facade: Gagg's Hill Shop, St Joseph, on the way to Bathsheba. Sue Hume

Nigel Benn Aunty Bar
Shorey Village, St Andrew

If you've gone trekking through the wilds of St Andrew, and all those sand dunes and Atlantic breezes have your throat a bit dry, stop at Nigel Benn Aunty Bar in Shorey Village just before the turn off to go up to Farley Hill Park.

Lucille Hall, the aunt of Barbadian-British middleweight boxer Nigel Benn, runs the bar and is a most welcoming hostess. The walls are covered in photos of her favourite nephew as well as those of celebrities and visitors. She serves a variety of snacks and keeps her drinks ice cold. Don't miss it.

Lucille Hall, proprietor and aunt of boxer Nigel Benn. Sue Hume

Ah… just hits the spot!
A patron of Nigel Benn Aunty Bar. Sue Hume

Nigel Benn Aunty Bar, Shorey Village, St Andrew. Sue Hume

Nigel Benn Aunty Bar. Sue Hume

Anderson Layne Shop
Chimborazo, St Joseph

This rum shop has been perched on top of Chimborazo for the past hundred years and looks like it has every intention of staying there for another hundred.

It's a traditional rural rum shop fronted by a cool verandah. The inside has been converted mainly to a bar, although it still sells convenience items.

On weekends chicken, fish and pork are available, and customers regularly play dominoes and cards.

Next time you're passing through scenic Chimborazo, stop for one. This is one of the highest rum shops in Barbados.

Anderson Layne Shop, Chimborazo, St Joseph: a traditional rural rum shop with verandah. Sue Hume

Cooling out on the verandah at Anderson Layne Shop, Chimborazo, St Joseph. Sue Hume

John Moore Bar
Weston, St James

A very popular hangout on the beach at Weston, St James, is John Moore Bar; the proprietor is L. Addison.

With a traditional shop front giving on to the road, and a large back room bordering the beach, this rum shop can accommodate a large number of patrons and usually does. Fish is a speciality of the house.

Any time of the day or night, you'll find this place buzzing.

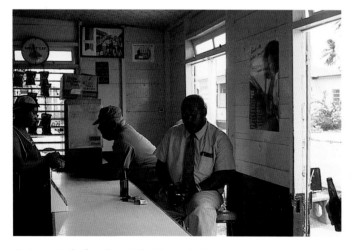

Customers in the front bar at John Moore's. Sue Hume

John Moore Bar, Weston, St James. Sue Hume

The signs speak for themselves: John Moore Bar. Sue Hume

Cooling out in the back at John Moore Bar. Sue Hume

Carie's Bar
Hillaby, St Thomas

Run by an enterprising young woman, Pamela Clarke, Carie's Bar is a popular rum shop in Hillaby. Colourfully painted, spacious and clean, this rum shop has a large bar with a pool room next door.

Carie's also serves lunches. The food is tasty and includes chicken and fish and a variety of cutters, and souse and breadfruit on Saturdays.

This is also one of the highest rum shops in Barbados. No visit to Mount Hillaby, the highest point in Barbados, is complete without a stop at Carie's.

Carie's Bar, Hillaby, St Thomas. Sue Hume

Shooting pool at Carie's Bar, Hillaby. Sue Hume

Inside Carie's Bar. Sue Hume

Hendy's Bus Stop Bar and Grocery, Ruby Main Road, St Philip. **Maxie Baldeo**

Hendy's Bus Stop Bar
Ruby Main Road, St Philip

If you're driving to Sam Lord's Castle don't fail to stop at Hendy's Bus Stop Bar and Grocery on the Ruby Main Road opposite Hilda Skeete Primary School.

Whether because of its convenient location at the junction, or because the owner, Henderson Linton, and his helpers are such genial hosts, this watering hole is always bustling.

This rum shop has been in the Linton family for generations. It's popular with patrons from near and far, and many a weary traveller from Bridgetown en route to the wilds of St Philip has refreshed himself there. Conversation, rum and beer flow freely.

Besides the drinks on offer in the well-stocked bar, ham, cheese and fish cutters are available daily. On weekends the speciality is barbecued chicken and breadfruit fries.

Propping up the bar at Hendy's. **Maxie Baldeo**

The Almond Tree Bar
East Point Road, St Philip

This gem is but a long stone's throw from Ragged Point lighthouse. Proprietor Beryl Mason and her husband have been running it successfully since 1981.

This classic, cosy, two-door shop is one of the smallest in Barbados. Behind it, however, is a large room with chairs and tables where the owners do a thriving trade in lunches for workmen from nearby businesses as well as minibus drivers and passers-by, including tourists. The rice and stew is tasty and the pork chops are out of this world. They also serve pudding and souse on Saturdays.

Domino competitions take place regularly in the back room.

It's a bright and breezy shop, and if you feel like it, you can lounge out under the large almond tree that shades the shop, sipping a long, cold one.

This is definitely a rum shop not to be missed.

Mr Mason behind the bar of the Almond Tree. Maxie Baldeo

The Almond Tree Bar, Ragged Point, St Philip. **Maxie Baldeo**

Londun Bar
Silver Sands, Christ Church

The Londun Bar, located opposite the beach at Silver Sands, is a favourite hangout for people from all over the island, especially on Friday nights. The reason is not hard to find. There is a mouth-watering variety of seafood including bill fish, chub, jacks, octopus, conch and sea eggs. The atmosphere is congenial, and host Graham Nurse makes sure everyone has a good time.

Nurse has been in the fishing business a lifetime, and has taught fishing. He was recently awarded the Silver Star of Merit. He enjoys keeping the bar, though it is hard going.

Although not a traditional rum shop, Londun Bar exemplifies the true spirit of the rum shop. Don't miss it.

View of the sea from Londun Bar, Silver Sands, Christ Church. Maxie Baldeo

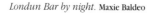

Londun Bar by night. Maxie Baldeo

The proprietor of Londun Bar, Graham Nurse. Maxie Baldeo

The Fisherman's Pub
Queen Street, Speightstown, St Peter

The Fisherman's Pub and Beach Bar is a popular watering hole on the West Coast. Here is a fine example of a rum shop that grew to become a pub and restaurant catering to visitors and locals alike.

Proprietor Clement Armstrong has been operating this rum shop since 1972 and has enlarged it from a hole in the wall to a spacious beach restaurant offering a variety of local foods at very reasonable prices. The menu includes fish, cou cou and salt fish, breadfruit, split peas and rice, sweet potatoes and Black Belly lamb.

There is karaoke on Mondays and a live band on Wednesday evenings.

Despite the expansion into a restaurant and bar this is one rum shop that has not lost its soul – a must-see if you're in Speightstown.

The Fisherman's Pub, Speightstown, St Peter. Maxie Baldeo

The deck at the Fisherman's Pub. Maxie Baldeo

Proprietor Clement Armstrong at the Fisherman's Pub. Maxie Baldeo

The restaurant in the Fisherman's Pub. Maxie Baldeo

Braddie's Bar
Dover, Christ Church

Located near to the Dover playing field in the St Lawrence area, just off the Top Rock roundabout, Braddie's is one of the most popular rum shops in Barbados.

You will find a fascinating mix of people, a great atmosphere, and mouth-watering chicken wings, pork chops and other delicacies.

Longstanding politician Delisle Bradshaw and his wife run this lively bar. Weekends are peak times, especially Friday nights when the bar stays open to the early hours of the morning. If you're in the neighbourhood, remember to call in at Braddie's.

A front view of Braddie's. Orlando Marville

Friday evenings are always busy at Braddie's Bar. Orlando Marville

Braddie's Bar, Dover, Christ Church. Orlando Marville

Grantley's Shop
Coach Hill, St John

Grantley's is perched on the hill leading down to Bath Beach and commands a panoramic view of the St John coast. Owner Grantley Haynes serves up a delicious variety of food, including, of course, fish, pork chops, cutters, breadfruit fries and on Saturdays, souse.

Grantley's is a great place to relax and have a cool drink. The shop has a jukebox with golden oldies. If you want to throw a party this is a great place to do it.

Grantley's Shop, Coach Hill, St John. Orlando Marville

Customers on the verandah of Grantley's. Orlando Marville

The view of the St John coast from Grantley's. Orlando Marville

Hammie's Shop
Long Gap, Spooners Hill, St Michael

If you're visiting Tyrol Cot, the historic home of Sir Grantley Adams, go down the hill a little way and turn into Long Gap. There you'll find the best ham cutters in the world at Hammie's Shop.

Proprietor Hamilton Hoyte who has been running the shop for 18 years has a faithful clientele who come not only for the food and drink but also for the congenial company.

Hammie's Shop, Long Gap, Spooners Hill. Orlando Marville

Food storage bin at Hammie's.
Orlando Marville

Customers liming outside Hammie's. Orlando Marville

Babe's Bar
Lower Estate Road, St George

Babe's Bar is a recently renovated rum shop located on the Lower Estate Road not far from Charles Rowe Bridge. Owner Clovine Price serves macaroni pie, baked chicken, fried fish and a variety of cutters – all very tasty.

Thursday night is karaoke night. Babe's also has a pool room at the back and ample parking. It is becoming increasingly popular and has a warm friendly atmosphere – definitely not to be missed.

Incidentally, a little further along the road, opposite the sports pavilion, lives Hazel Alleyne, a pillar of her church and the best pudding and souse maker in Barbados!

Babe's Bar, Lower Estate Road, St George. Orlando Marville

Inside Babe's Bar. Orlando Marville

The pool room at Babe's. Orlando Marville

Babe's Bar. Orlando Marville

Bibliography

Barbados Rum Book. London: Macmillan Caribbean, 1985.

Barry-King, Hugh and Massel, Antony, *Rum Yesterday and Today*. London: Heinemann, 1983.

Brathwaite, Jewel, 'Progress Changes the Village Shops', *Sunday Advocate*, 20 December 1987.

Callender, Wendell, 'Rum Shop Talk', *Daily Nation*, 5 January 2000.

Carter, Henderson, 'A History of the Rum Enterprise in Barbados, 1640–1815'. M.Phil thesis, University of the West Indies, Cave Hill, 1993.

Corbin, Oswald, 'The Social and Economic Roles of Village Shops in Barbados as Illustrated in the Case Study of Todd's and Macaroni Villages, St. George, 1930–1990'. Caribbean Studies Thesis, University of the West Indies, Cave Hill, 1992.

Faria, Norman, 'Village Shops Barely Hanging in There', *Advocate*, 4 November 1991.

Gittens, Terri, 'Rum Shops Now Clean and Bright', *Weekend Investigator*, 17 September 1993.

Harris, Margaret Ann, 'The Village Shop – End of a Barbadian Era?', *Sunday Advocate*, 14 March 1999.

Hughes, Ronald, 'St Elizabeth's Village, St Joseph', *Journal of the Barbados Museum and Historical Society*, March 1979, Vol. XXXVI, No. 1.

King, Courtney, 'Vital Role of Village Shops', *Sunday Advocate News*, 7 May 1978.

Mclellan, H.H., 'Barbados Back in Time: The Way We Were'. Demarara: The Argosy, 1909.

Marshall, Woodville, 'Villages and Plantation Sub-Division', in *Emancipation III: Aspects of the Post-Slavery Experience in Barbados,* ed. W. Marshall. Bridgetown: University of the West Indies, 1988.

Richardson, Bonham, *Panama Money in Barbados, 1900–1920*. Knoxville: University of Tennessee Press, 1985.

Stoute, Janet and Ifill, Kenneth, 'The Rural Rum Shop', in *Everyday Life in Barbados: A Sociological Perspective,* ed. Graham Dann. The Hague, 1976.

Stuart, Juliet, 'The Changing Features of the Village Shop'. Caribbean Studies Thesis, University of the West Indies, Cave Hill, 1997.